# IS PHOTOPACK THE HOME FRONT 1939–1945

Tony D Triggs

**Ideas pages**



**Copiable pages**



Folens Publishers

# INTRODUCTION



The extract from the letter from Miss Verney (page 5) is taken from the Ministry of Information records INF 1/266 1940. The information on page 15 is adapted from 'Beating the Invader: A message from the Prime Minister', INF 3/219, issued by the Ministry of Information in 1940.

Editor: Alison Millar

Layout artist: Patricia Hollingsworth

Illustrations by: Jeremy Bays/ Graham-Cameron Illustration

Cover by: In Touch Creative Services Ltd

First published 1995 by Folens Limited, Dunstable and Dublin.

ISBN 1 85276 690-5

Folens Limited, Albert House, Apex Business Centre, Boscombe Road, Dunstable, LU5 4RL, England.

Folens Publishers

The purpose of this Photopack is to stimulate interest in and historical enquiry into the lives of ordinary people during an important period of British history: 1939–1945. The photographs have been chosen to give a strong visual impression of life at the time and can be used as starting points for activities and discussion in the classroom.

Children puzzled by what they see in the photographs have already had their interest engaged and this can lead them to ask further questions of people who can remember the war years: What was it like to be evacuated? What was it like during the Blitz?

By investigating the copious printed and oral sources of information for the wartime years, the children will soon identify discrepancies and will have the stimulus of trying to explain and reconcile them. Thus, the process of gathering information and evidence will lead them to function as true historians, sifting, evaluating, comparing, arranging and finding cause and consequence.

Like other primary and secondary sources, photographs show bias, selectivity and manipulation and this is frequently highlighted in the teachers' notes. The children should become aware of this as they work their way through the activities.

Photographs give a human face to things of the past, aiding involvement and empathy even without the help of living witnesses. Being non-verbal, they also serve the needs of all abilities. Their breadth of appeal, along with the suggested activities and teaching strategies in this pack, should make them a valuable resource for teaching this area of history in the primary classroom.

The photographs can be used for research, raising questions such as: 'What is shown?' and 'Where is this taking place?' To facilitate this, the description of each photograph is contained in the teachers' notes and not on the photograph.

This pack also contains ten miniature reproductions of the photographs and a large colour poster. These could be used by the children as they are working on projects, for example, as a reference while researching the subject, for sequencing or for work in pairs. Alternatively, they could be used as the centrepiece in a collection of the children's work in the class project-book or display.

# EVACUATION

Photo 1 © The Hulton Deutsch Collection.

At the start of the war, the British government decided that children living in the likely target areas for German bombing should be evacuated to foster homes in villages and country towns.

While parents were free to keep their children at home if they wished, many sent their children away but fetched them back within a few months.

Evacuation was often carried out on a school-by-school basis. Teachers went away with their pupils and tried to re-establish the school. Children who stayed behind in the cities sometimes found there was no school to go to.

The photograph shows evacuee children from London boarding buses on 1 September 1939.

## *Starting points*

- Give the children the exact date of the photograph and discuss the purpose of evacuation.
- Explain how experience of World War I made people fear gas in World War II. Ask the children if they can see signs of gas masks in the photograph.
- Ask them to look at the evacuees' faces for signs of what they might be feeling.
- How might the German public have felt if they had seen this photograph at the time?
- What possessions might the evacuated children have wanted to take with them? What might today's children want to take with them?

## *Key questions*

1. What is happening in the photograph?
2. What are the children carrying? Why?
3. Are the evacuees near the start of their journey or near its end? (Point out the relative lack of adults, suggesting that their parents have already seen them off.)

## *Activities*

- Ask each child to identify with one of the children in the photograph and imagine meeting their foster family. They could write a postcard or letter to tell their parents about their journey and how they are feeling. The children could start by making a list like the one on the right.

| Feelings | Reason |
|---|---|
| Loneliness | My parents are miles away. |
| Fear | By myself for the first time. |
| Excitement | Seeing the countryside for the first time. |

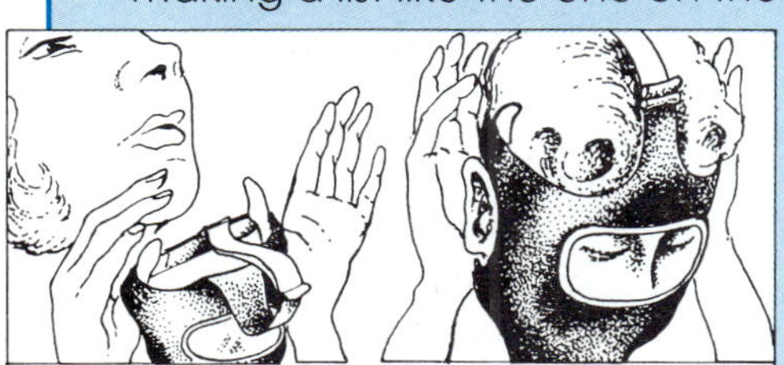
1. Hold your breath. 2. Hold mask in front of face, with thumbs inside straps.
3. Thrust chin well forward into mask, pull straps over head as far as they will go.
4. Run finger round face-piece taking care head-straps are not twisted.

- The children could design a poster encouraging parents to send their children into the countryside. They could start by discussing the example above.
- Groups of children could interview grandparents, or other people they know, about their experiences of evacuation. If the accounts disagree with each other, or with the photograph, the children should discuss the reasons.

# THE HOME GUARD

Photo 2 © The Hulton Deutsch Collection.

The government, fearing a German invasion, stressed the need for every town to have trained volunteers who could hinder this. The regular army would then have time to reach the scene.

Bands of Local Defence Volunteers (LDVs) were formed throughout the country. Also known as the Home Guard, the volunteers had ordinary jobs by day and trained in the evening or at weekends. Most of the volunteers were those too old for conscription, or not fit for military service.

In the event, the Germans did not land in mainland Britain, so the Home Guard did not have to go into action.

The photograph shows LDVs in training on 21 June 1940.

## *Starting points*

- Ask the children to discuss how the men on the ground have positioned their bodies (including their legs).
- Ask the children to discuss the mood (or moods) of the onlookers in the photograph. Point out the man at the rear who is looking away. What might this indicate?
- What do the trainees' clothes and ages suggest about how their Home Guard training fitted into their lives?
- If the children only had this picture, what conclusions might they draw about the defence of Britain?

## *Key questions*

1. What is happening in the photograph? What sort of place is being used?
2. What are the bricks for?
3. What might the man with binoculars be looking at?
4. Besides the man in uniform, there is one other soldier. Which man is it? How can you tell?
5. Why are there no women present in the photograph?

## *Activities*

| The German idea | The British reply |
|---|---|
| Britain's army weak so must have old men to defend the country. | All British citizens prepared to fight for their country. |

- Ask the children to imagine that a German spy has taken the photograph of the Home Guard. Then ask them to use it as the basis of a report making fun of British war preparations. The children could list and rebut the key points of the report in a chart such as the one above right.
- Ask the children to study the map on page 14 and identify points that would be of special concern for local defence. For example, where would lookout points be built or established? Where (and why) might anti-glider ditches be dug? What about the pier?

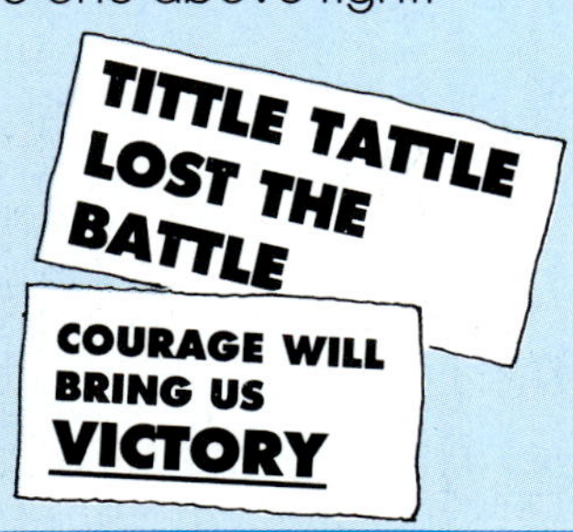


- Introduce the idea of propaganda and the fact that the government published much material for this purpose. Discuss the government's advice for dealing with a German invasion (page 15). What was the reason for each instruction? What could have been the consequences of ignoring them?

# ENTERTAINMENT

**Photo 3 © The Hulton Deutsch Collection.**

Gracie Fields (on the ladder in the photograph) was one of the most famous singers of the wartime years and often entertained troops and workers with her rousing and reassuring songs.

The entertainment industry was a vital part of the British war effort. Songs like *There'll Always be an England* maintained the determination to win, while *Heil, Hitler, yah, yah, yah, Oh what a horrid little man you are* belittled the German leader.

Television broadcasts stopped for the duration of the war so BBC radio was the main source of entertainment, information and propaganda.

## *Starting points*

- How could the feelings of ordinary people affect how Britain fared in the war?
- At the start of the war the government set up the Ministry of Information which told the media what to say about the conflict. Ask the children to consider why the government did this.
- Help the children to understand the dangers of censorship. Why should truth often be 'the first casualty of war'?

## *Key questions*

1. Where was the photograph taken? What is happening?
2. How are the men looking at the singer? What might this suggest about how they feel about her?
3. Why are the people in these positions? Is there any reason to think that the picture is posed?

## *Activities*

- Reproduce the letter on the right which was sent to the Ministry of Information and ask the children to study it. Ask them to decide what sort of work Miss Verney did. They could think of alternative names for the Ministry, including some that would have appealed to Miss Verney or the people she worked with.
- The children could write a reply that the Ministry might have sent to Miss Verney.
- Ask the children to find out about Lord Haw-Haw (William Joyce). They could then write and record conflicting British and German news reports concerned with some event or aspect of the war. Pose the question: 'When does entertainment become propaganda?'.

Dear Sir,

I work in one of our biggest armaments factories and on all sides I hear discussions going on. I cannot put into words what they say about the BBC ... they call me all sorts of fools for believing you, and I find nine out of every ten of them listen to Lord Haw-Haw, saying they can get more truth from him, and they want me to do the same ... It is a standing joke in our factory about your oft-repeated phrase, 'all our planes returned safely' ... Really I am so bewildered by all they say that I do not know what to believe. I feel I must listen to German news now, or I cannot argue unless I know the two sides.

Yours truly, Miss Verney

| Title | Fact | Opinion |
|---|---|---|
| There'll Always be an England | | |
| Heil, Hitler ... | | |

- One side in the war had a song which went: 'Have you any stinking fish, Britannia dear?'. Children could decide which side would have sung it and make up additional lines to complete at least one verse.
- Children could research and examine the titles and words of British wartime songs and decide whether the main ingredient is fact or opinion.

# WOMEN AT WORK

**Photo 4 © The Hulton Deutsch Collection.**

Poster campaigns encouraged women to work in factories, especially those that made aircraft and other war materials.

Women workers replaced the men who had been conscripted into the forces. Their work was vital to the British war effort. In the words of a popular song of the time:

> It's the girl that makes the thing that
> drills the hole that holds the spring
> That works the thingumebob that
> makes the engines roar.
> And it's the girl that makes the thing
> that holds the oil that oils the thing
> That works the thingumebob THAT'S
> GOING TO WIN THE WAR.

By July 1943, all women not taking care of children under 14 years old had to do some form of war work.

The photograph shows a woman involved in munitions work. The unusual use of colour suggests that this is a propaganda photograph.

## *Starting points*

- Describe the woman's clothing. Why is she dressed like this?
- If the woman had met her counterpart from a German factory, what various feelings might they have expressed?
- Ask the children to discuss the 'thingumebob' song and list a few of the ideas behind it, such as: 'To win the war we all need to do our bit'.

## *Key questions*

1. What is the woman doing?
2. What would her working conditions have been like?
3. Who would have worked in factories such as this before the war?
4. What effects might working have had on women's home lives?
5. How would children have had to adapt?

## *Activities*

- The children could take the role of the woman in the photograph, writing to let her husband in the forces know all about her new job and how the family's life has changed.
- Show the 'Attack Begins in the Factory' poster and ask the children to think of a caption for the 'woman worker' photograph so that it would have the same message.
- The children could research the kinds of jobs that women did during the war and assess which were the most important and why. Ask them whether they think looking after children was more important than making munitions.
- More research could be carried out about if and how women's work roles changed after 1945. Is it true to say that World War II was the real beginning of women's independence?

# FOOD SUPPLY

Photo 5 © The Imperial War Museum, London.

German U-boats sank cargo ships bringing food and other vital supplies across the Atlantic, so some foods became scarce and had to be rationed.

To increase home production, some women volunteered to work on the land. They became the Women's Land Army (or simply the 'land girls'). They managed to increase farm production, but not enough to compensate for the fall in imports.

The 'Dig for Victory' campaign encouraged families to grow their own produce in place of imported foodstuffs.

Because of food shortages, the government developed a poster campaign. The photograph shows a poster from 1941.

## *Starting points*

- Help the children to understand what risk the British government would run if people could not get enough food.
- Discuss how 'digging for victory' could work.
- The myth that carrots help people see in the dark was originated during the war by the Ministry of Food who claimed that they would help people to see during the blackout. Discuss with the children why the Ministry of Food should have created such a myth.
- Ask the children to think of some words for the 'pot luck' poster that say the same thing in a different way.

## *Key questions*

1. Which wartime leaders are identified on the poster?
2. What is the poster saying about these two leaders?
3. What advice and what threat does the poster contain?

'Potato Pete', one of the popular characters created by the Ministry of Food for their nutrition campaign.

## *Activities*

- Ask the children to study a typical family's pre-war menu, as shown above. Ask them to research which foods on the sheet came from overseas, which countries they came from and how (and by which routes) they were imported. They could research how and where the Germans cut Britain's food supply line.
- The children could adapt the menu to show any changes needed because of the war.

| Food before 1939 | Why was there a change? | Alternatives |
|---|---|---|
| Bananas<br>Sugar<br>Apricots | Came from the West Indies.<br><br>Trade routes blocked. | 'Dig for Victory'.<br><br>Grow your own fruit, but not tropical fruit.<br><br>Ration some foods. |

- Challenge the children to take on the role of a German designing handbills to drop from aircraft over Britain. A possible theme is food. The children could consider adapting the 'pot luck' poster so that the message in some way favours the Germans.

# THE BLITZ

Photo 6 © The Hulton Deutsch Collection.

There were two main phases of German bombing: from September 1940 to May 1941, known as the Blitz, and from early 1944 to the spring of 1945.

The British detected approaching planes in time to set off air-raid sirens which sent people scurrying into their shelters. Anti-aircraft guns provided some protection but the best defence was the blackout.

Wardens patrolled each district to make sure people were obeying the blackout regulations and to organise rescues after each air raid.

The photograph shows the result of bombing in London on 19 September 1940.

## *Starting points*

- Discuss with the children why the Germans attacked cities such as London. What other sites did they attack regularly and why?
- The Germans sometimes fixed whistles to their bombs, causing them to screech as they fell. Ask the children to suggest a possible reason. This could lead to discussion of why the Germans bombed civilian areas, as well as areas directly concerned with Britain's ability to fight the war. Did the Allies ever behave in this way?
- Discuss which local sites were targets of German bombing (or would have been targets if they had bombed the area).

## *Key questions*

1. In relation to the area shown in the photograph, where does the bomb appear to have fallen?
2. What signs of the blackout can the children see?
3. Which man is a warden and which is a soldier? How can you tell?
4. Why are no people coming to stare at the damage?

## *Activities*

- The photograph appeared in a British newspaper. One group of children could play the role of journalists and write a news report to go with it. Making notes will help.
- Ask another group what the Germans would have thought of the photograph. They could write the sort of reports that might have appeared in a German paper. The children could compare the 'slants' of their reports and give reasons for any differences in them.

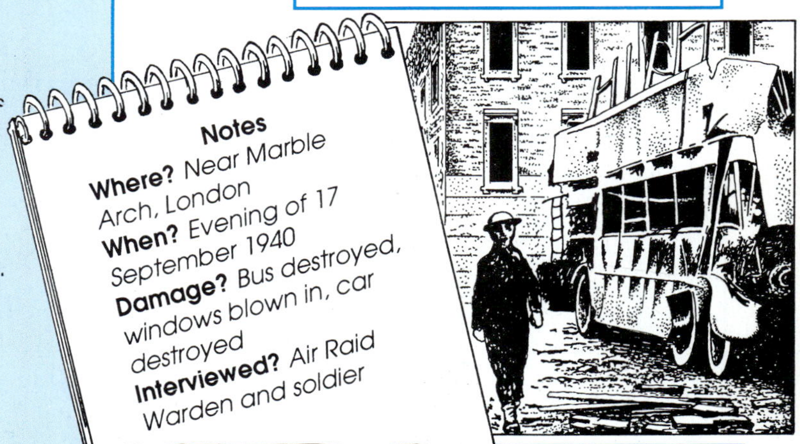


| Danger/Problem | Solution |
|---|---|
| Flying glass | Use heavy curtains and put tape over windows. |
| Gas leaks | Don't smoke. |

- Ask the children to draw up a table listing the dangers and problems of the Blitz and ways of combating them.
- Roleplay a scene in which someone is just back from overseas and a warden or neighbour is explaining all the safety measures necessary when dealing with an air raid.

 

# RATIONING

Photo 7 © The Hulton Deutsch Collection.

In 1941, clothes joined food and petrol among the things that were rationed.

Everyone had 66 clothing coupons to last a year, each garment 'costing' a number of coupons as well as its usual price in money. The government fixed the number of coupons required for each item.

From March 1942, hardly any petrol was available for private motoring and very few cars were seen on the roads. Petrol supplied for farm vehicles and public transport was dyed red for identification purposes.

The photograph shows a shopper bringing her ration book to a shop assistant in Woolworth's on the first day of rationing, 3 June 1941.

## *Starting points*

- Ask the children to list the differences between the scene in the photograph and a scene in a clothes shop today.

| The shop in 1941 | A shop today |
| --- | --- |
| | |

- They could try to imagine the feelings and attitudes of people when they went shopping in 1941 with their ration books, compared with the feelings and attitudes of shoppers today.
- What evidence is there in the photograph of the cost of items? How much might they cost today?

## *Key questions*

1. What is the woman buying?
2. What is she handing to the assistant?
3. Why was there a need to ration certain items during the war?
4. What might have been some of the problems of living with rationing?

## *Activities*

- The children could interview grandparents or others who lived through the war and find out what it was like to cope with rationing, shortages and transport problems. Discuss the poster above.
- Study the lists of men's and women's garments on page 16 and discuss how clothing has changed since the war and why it has changed. Encourage the children to consider the ways in which the lists reflect the outlooks, attitudes and assumptions people had at the time. For example, why was the swimwear ration just for men and boys and the apron and pinafore ration just for women and girls?

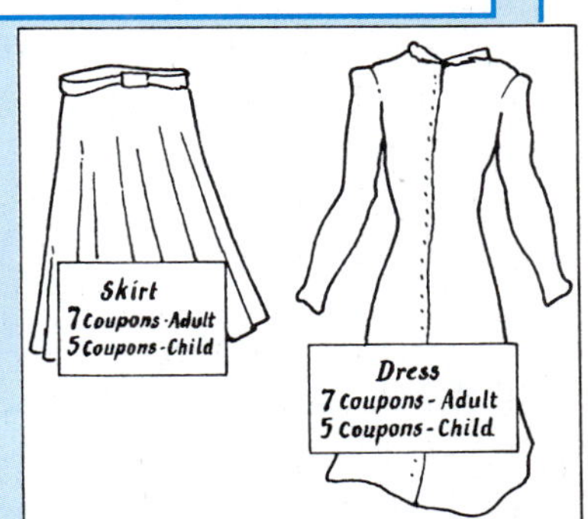


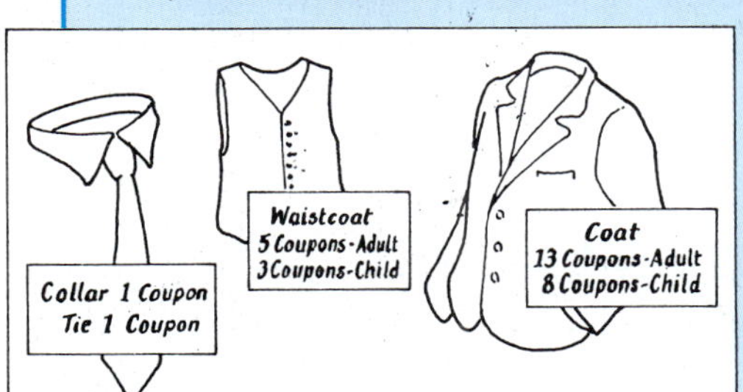


- The children could draw up a wartime shopping list, showing what they would have to buy in order to kit themselves out. The lists should show the number of coupons required for each item and the total compared with the quota of 66.
- They could then consider how long each item would last. Would they need new shoes within a year? They will almost certainly find themselves running out of coupons. How would they have coped during the war?

# AIR-RAID SHELTERS

Photo 8 © The Hulton Deutsch Collection.

By the start of the war, 50 per cent of British homes had air-raid shelters in their gardens. The government issued them free of charge to families living on low incomes and for £7 to the better off.

Known as Anderson shelters, after their inventor, they were made from corrugated steel and they looked a little like railway tunnels. They had to be set in dug-outs which were almost as deep as the shelter was high (about two metres). Soil was then heaped over the shelter to a depth of up to half a metre. Entry was via a sloping trench.

Some air-raid shelters were built from brick. They stood above ground and the roofs consisted of a single bomb-proof concrete slab.

The photograph, dated 21 September 1940, shows a family from South London who luckily escaped death when the local warden discovered a delayed action bomb near their shelter.

| Item | Reason for use |
|---|---|
| Candles | No electricity supply and blackout. |
| Blankets | Cold at night – no heating. |
| Books | Boring waiting for 'all-clear' to sound. |

## *Starting points*

- Discuss with the children what an Anderson shelter would protect people from.
- Help the children to imagine the discomforts of using an Anderson shelter. How large is it? How warm might it have been? How would it be lit? What items would a family keep in their shelter or take there with them? Why would heavy rain be a problem?
- The government wanted to make the shelters as popular as possible. What sort of pictures or news reports would they have banned or discouraged?

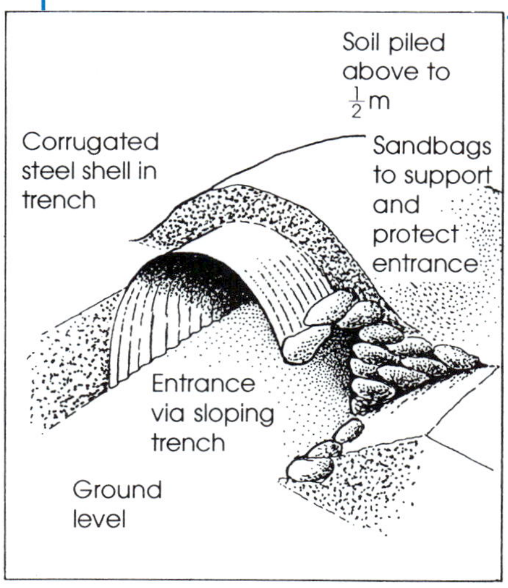


## *Key questions*

1. Why is so much of the shelter showing? What might this suggest about the state the family's home is in?
2. What is the 'message' of the photograph?
3. How might the photograph influence families who saw it in their local newspaper?

## *Activities*

- Ask the children to think about the shape of the Anderson air-raid shelter. In particular, why did it have a curved top? The children could experiment using flat sheets of cardboard and then corrugated cardboard to make domed and flat-topped shapes. Which shape is stronger? Which type of cardboard is stronger?
- Despite having bomb-proof roofs, the free-standing brick-built shelters were not very safe. Challenge the children to think what the problems with such shelters might have been.
- Ask them to find out what other places people used as shelters in London and other big cities.
- List the items people might have taken with them into the shelters during an air raid. What might be stored in them and why? Answers could be shown on a chart like the one on the left.

 

# A ROYAL VISIT

Photo 9 © The Hulton Deutsch Collection.

Many Londoners had their homes destroyed and some began spending their nights in the underground stations. Other Londoners used the stations as air-raid shelters. The stations became so overcrowded that some people slept on the railway tracks after the power had been turned off for the night.

In the first phase of bombing, the poorer eastern parts of London suffered more than the districts further west. This led to unrest, with 'East-enders' claiming that the government should provide more care for the victims.

The photograph shows King George VI and Queen Elizabeth (now the Queen Mother) visiting bombed-out people in an underground station on 14 November 1940. Gestures like this gained them public respect, as did the fact that they stayed in the London area instead of going somewhere safer during the Blitz.

| Person | Role or activity | Reasons |
|---|---|---|
| Princess Elizabeth | In the Land Army. | Working like other women. |
| Churchill | Making the victory sign. | Giving people hope of winning. |
| King George | In uniform with his troops. | A fighting soldier like others. |

## *Starting points*

- Discuss with the children what it would have been like living in an underground station. Consider fresh air, toilets, comfort, safety, light and privacy.
- Ask the children to consider the factors that could have depressed people, such as shortage of food and lack of sleep. Which of these could the government relieve and how?
- How could visits by royalty and politicians cheer up people living in an underground station?

**Recording an Interview**

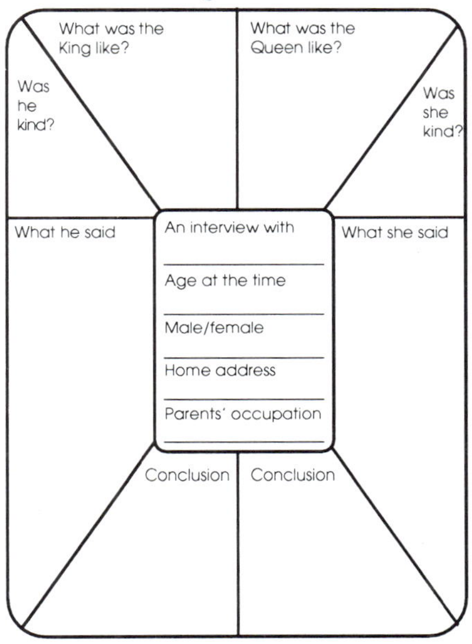


## *Key questions*

1. Where was the photograph taken?
2. Why are the people there?
3. How can you tell who the King and Queen are?
4. What do the people seem to think of the visit?
5. How suitable was the King and Queen's choice of clothes for their visit? Why?
6. What does the photograph say about the success of the evacuation policy?

## *Activities*

- The children could list some questions they might have wanted to ask the King and Queen, for example, 'Are you hungry like us?'. They could also suggest the answers.
  - They could role-play interviewing one of the people who met the King and Queen. They could use an interview sheet such as the one shown above.
  - The children could describe the visit from the viewpoint of the King or Queen, either in a letter or a diary entry.
  - Challenge the children to collect photographs of the royal family and other British and German leaders from this period. They should note the roles and activities that are shown or omitted and the image that is being presented. Suggest reasons for these. They could list their findings on a chart like the one opposite.

# TWO FACES OF WAR

Photos 10 & 11, © The Hulton Deutsch Collection.

This page provides ideas for activities that use two of the pictures in this pack, one showing the tragic results of the bombing in Coventry in November 1940 and the other showing a soldier named Tim returning home from the war.

In the graveyard scene, the coffins of 172 victims have been lowered into long trenches. To save on wood, many wartime coffins were made from papier mâché or cardboard. The cardboard ones were collapsible and large numbers of them were stored, ready for use.

In June 1944, British morale rose when the D-Day landings in Normandy established a second front in Europe. Victory in Europe came on 8 May 1945 and many troops were demobilised shortly afterwards, returning home to rapturous welcomes.

## *Starting points*

- Compare the two photographs. Discuss with the children whether the photographer influenced the people's behaviour in either of the pictures.
- Ask the children which photograph they think might have appeared in a newspaper of the time and which might have appeared in a personal album?
- Is there any evidence to suggest that the photographs were posed for a purpose?
- What were D-Day and VE Day? How did they get their names?

## *Key questions*

1. How does the background of the graveyard picture help to show that there were many victims and many mourners?
2. In both pictures, people have chosen a similar way to show their patriotism. What is it?
3. What are the people in the 'Soldier Tim' picture celebrating?
4. Look at the way the soldier's child has turned its head. What might this indicate?
5. What two faces of war are being shown in the photographs?

## *Activities*

- Look at Tim's child in the 'welcome home' photograph. As he grew up, Tim and his mother probably wanted to tell him all about the war. Working in pairs, the children could list on a chart things they might have shown him to help him to understand what people went through during the wartime years.

| Object | What it shows |
|---|---|
| Gas mask | People were afraid of dying in gas attacks. |
| Ration book | Many food items were in short supply. |
| Evacuation label | Children were sent away. |

- Some children could create a front page article covering the celebrations as demobilised soldiers return from the front. Others could create one about the other face of war, the despair after the bombing of a city. Compare the two.

 

# AN EVACUEE

- Imagine that you are to be evacuated in 1939. You can take only one small suitcase. What will you take with you and why?

Evacuee's name:

Date of birth:

Destination:

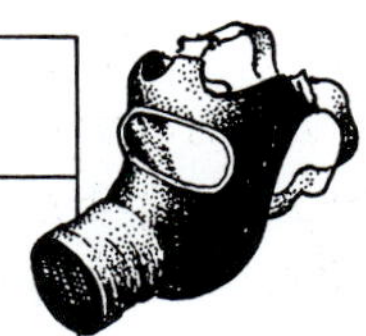

| What I would take | Why |
|---|---|
| | |

- Compare your list with a partner's. Explain any differences.

# DEFEND THE TOWN

- Work in groups to study this map of an imaginary town in 1941. You are in charge of the Home Guard. Identify any points that would be of special concern for local defence.
  - Which parts would be attacked first? Why?
  - Where would lookout points be built?
  - Where and why might anti-glider ditches be dug?
  - What other precautions would you take?
  - What about the pier?

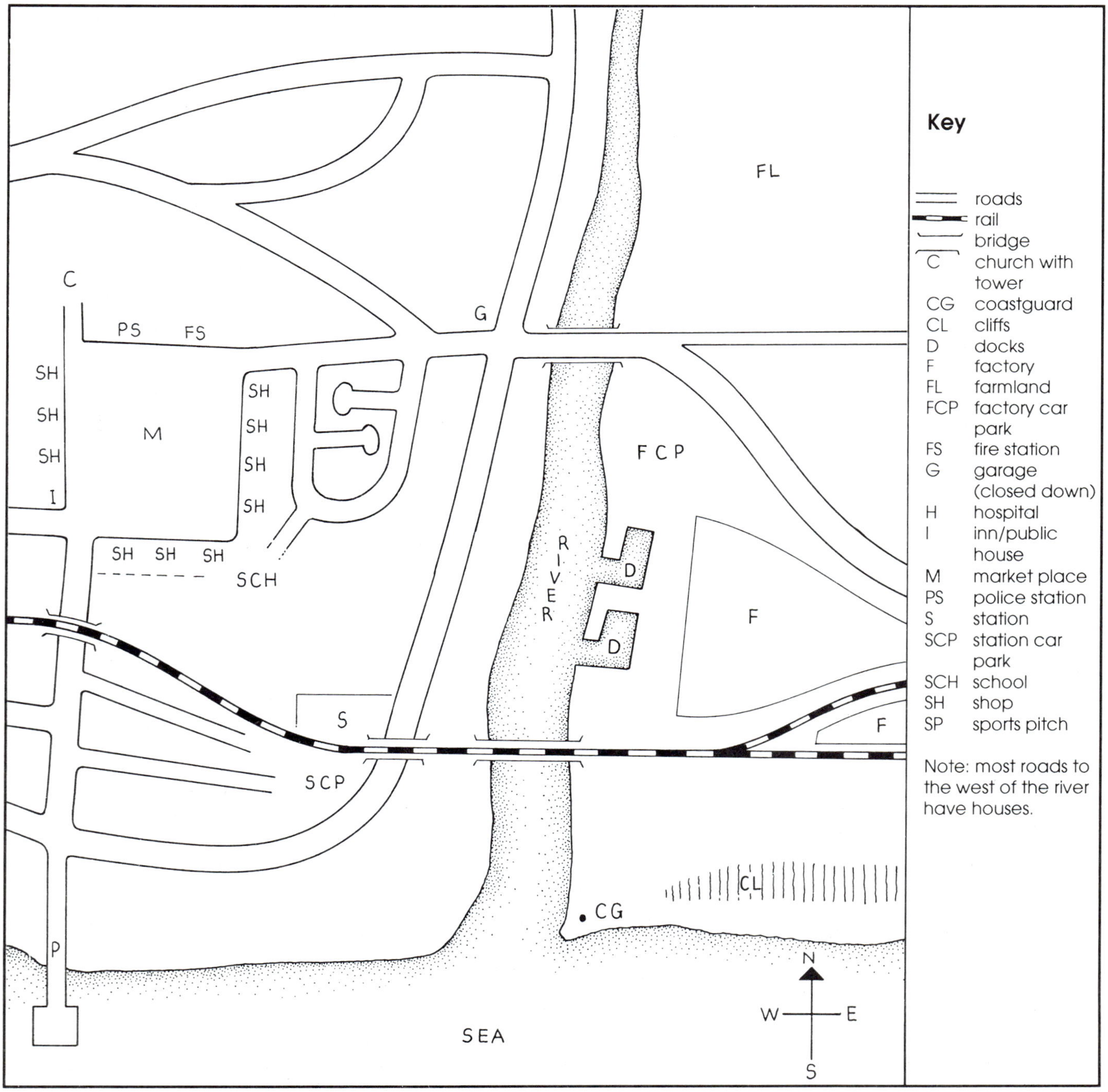


 

# INVASION!

- Discuss the government's advice for dealing with a possible German invasion.
  What was the reason for each instruction?
  What might have happened if the instructions were ignored?

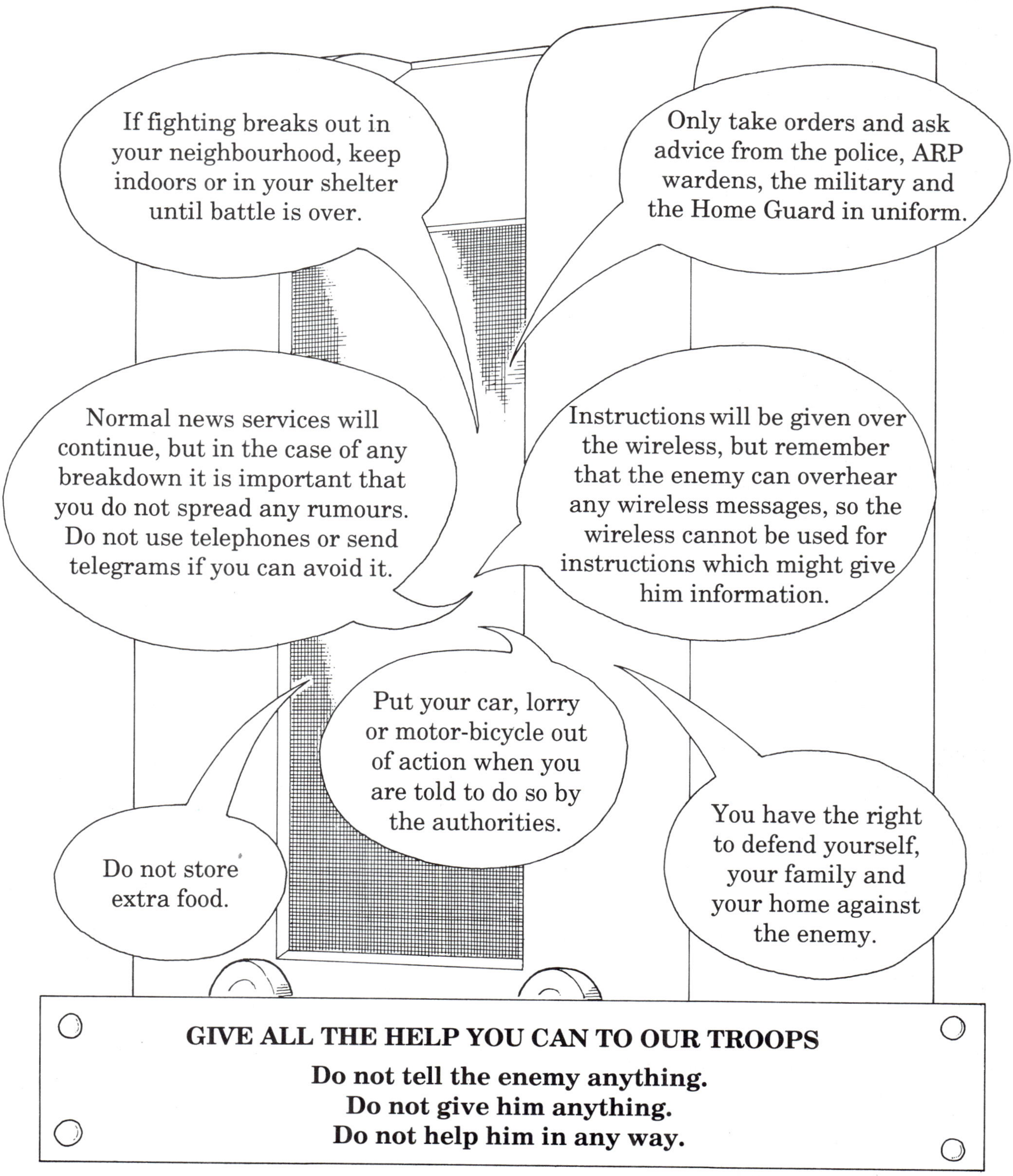

# CLOTHING RATIONS

- Study the clothing rations below.
  Work out what clothing you would need for a year.
  Would you have enough coupons? You only have 66 every year.

**Men and boys**

| | Adult | Child |
|---|---|---|
| Unlined mackintosh or cape | 9 | 7 |
| Other mackintoshes, or raincoat, or overcoat | 16 | 11 |
| Coat, or jacket, or blazer, or like garment | 13 | 8 |
| Waistcoat, or pullover, or cardigan, or jersey | 5 | 3 |
| Trousers (other than fustian or corduroy) | 8 | 6 |
| Fustian or corduroy trousers | 5 | 5 |
| Shorts | 5 | 3 |
| Overalls, or dungarees, or like garment | 6 | 4 |
| Dressing-gown or bathing-gown | 8 | 6 |
| Night-shirt or pair of pyjamas | 8 | 6 |
| Shirt or combinations – woollen | 8 | 6 |
| Shirt or combinations – other materials | 5 | 4 |
| Pants, or vest, or child's blouse | 4 | 2 |
| Pair of socks or stockings | 3 | 1 |
| Collar, or tie, or pair of cuffs | 1 | 1 |
| Two handkerchiefs | 1 | 1 |
| Scarf, or pair of gloves, or mittens | 2 | 2 |
| Pair of slippers or galoshes | 4 | 2 |
| Pair of boots or shoes | 7 | 3 |
| Pair of leggings, gaiters or spats | 3 | 2 |

**Women and girls**

| | Adult | Child |
|---|---|---|
| Lined mackintoshes, or coats (over 28 inches long) | 14 | 11 |
| Jacket, or short coat (under 28 inches long) | 11 | 8 |
| Dress, or gown, or frock – woollen | 11 | 8 |
| Dress, or gown, or frock – other material | 7 | 5 |
| Gym tunic, or girl's skirt with bodice | 8 | 6 |
| Blouse, or sports shirt, or cardigan, or jumper | 5 | 3 |
| Skirt, or divided skirt | 7 | 5 |
| Overalls, or dungarees, or like garment | 6 | 4 |
| Apron, or pinafore | 3 | 2 |
| Pyjamas | 8 | 6 |
| Night-dress | 6 | 5 |
| Petticoat, or slip, or combination, or cami-knickers | 4 | 3 |
| Other undergarments, including corsets | 3 | 2 |
| Pairs of stockings | 2 | 1 |
| Pairs of socks (ankle length) | 1 | 1 |
| Collar, or tie, or pair of cuffs | 1 | 1 |
| Two handkerchiefs | 1 | 1 |
| Scarf, or pair of gloves, or mittens, or muff | 2 | 2 |
| Pair of slippers, boots or shoes | 5 | 3 |
| Knitting wool (per two ounces) | 1 | 1 |

 